52 *SIMPLE WAYS*

TO MAKE

BUSINESS TRAVEL EASIER

C. E. Rollins

OLIVER
NELSON

THOMAS NELSON PUBLISHERS
Nashville

✦ Introduction

Despite the many wonderful technological advances made in recent years—including fax machines, teleconferencing, videotapes, one-hour photo processing, and overnight express delivery service—nothing seems to have been able to replace the value of a face-to-face encounter in conducting business. Personal presence is still important in making sales, brainstorming new projects and marketing ideas, reaching consensus, sharing information, bartering, and negotiating. The person-to-person handshake is still the mark of a "sealed deal."

Therefore, travel is still, and likely always will be, a part of business. Furthermore, the higher in an organization one finds oneself, the more likely it is that travel will be a routine part of the work schedule. If you're in business or if your career is on the rise, you probably can expect *more* travel in your future.

A person who travels routinely and extensively nearly always picks up tidbits of information that make the process easier. An idea here. A new way of doing things there.

This book is a collection of such ideas gathered

during more than twenty years of fairly extensive travel across the United States and Canada and to more than thirty other nations. I've also asked several other well-seasoned travelers—both men and women—to share their practical tips. Most of the ideas relate to travel by car or plane (commercial) and overnight lodging in hotels or motels. Those who travel by train, boat, bus, personal bus, or private plane—or who stay in private homes—will find many of the ideas adaptable to their modes of travel.

The suggestions here certainly are not definitive or exhaustive. You are invited to give them a try before adding them to your collection of travel tips. I trust, however, that they will make your business trips more fun, easier, more rewarding, and, in some cases, endurable.

Happy traveling!

1 ✦ Give Yourself Enough Time

Perhaps nothing wearies the business traveler more than hurrying up to wait.

Rushing is exhausting. The more starts and stops, the more revving up and slowing down, the more tiring any day or any trip will be.

Slow the Flow Try to maintain an even pace and flow to your personal motion—the gait of your walk, the way in which you lift items, the amount of energy you expend in hailing a cab.

Especially give yourself enough time in

- going to and from airports (train stations, bus stations, ship docks).

- getting to the next city.

- making it to the next appointment.

- making connecting flights or trains.

An even, unrushed pace will mean

- less perspiration.

- fewer spills.

- fewer things forgotten or left behind.

- less irritation with other travelers (who tend to get in your way).

- unpulled or unstrained muscles.

- fewer rips and tears.

- fewer broken nails and fewer hosiery snags and runs.

- fewer trips or falls.

All of those things tend to make you feel frazzled, worn out, and generally out of sync with the world. That isn't the mood you want to take with you into your next business appointment!

Schedule Wisely Many business travelers try to schedule too many appointments or do too many things in one eight-hour work day or one twenty-four-hour travel day.

Pace yourself. You'll last longer and retain a much more positive outlook on yourself, your business, and persons with whom you are meeting or working.

2 ✈ Choose Easy-Care Clothing

As much as possible, choose items of clothing that are wrinkle resistant, stain resistant, and washable. That way, you'll arrive at your business appointments looking fresher and feeling better about your appearance. You'll also spend far less hotel time worrying about steaming, pressing, or cleaning.

Take Off That Jacket As you travel by car or plane, hang up your jacket. It's a good idea even if you are only driving around the city on a series of appointments. You'll arrive at each place looking less crumpled.

Give Your Suit an Overnight Rest Alternate suits as you travel. Give one a chance to air out and hang out for a day while you wear the other. Your suits will last longer, and you'll spend far less time dealing with wrinkles.

Choose Knits Women travelers will find knits not only comfortable but wrinkle resistant.

Avoid Solid Colors in Smooth Fabrics for Jackets, Suits, Skirts, and Dresses Instead, choose tweeds, small prints, or fabrics with a subtle weave. Dirt and small stains won't be as noticeable.

Save Time and Money with Washable Fabrics
Choose garments that can be spot washed or
cleaned. Read labels closely. If in doubt, try washing or using a spot remover on a facing of the garment.

Go for a Loose Fit   Choose travel clothes that fit
loosely. Never travel in skintight garments. Many
people retain fluids as they travel, and if garments
are tight fitting at dawn, they'll be constricting and
misery causing by dusk! Choose garments with
elastic waists, loose armholes, and no restrictions
at the wrist. Women travelers should avoid girdles
and control-top panty hose (unless needed for
back support). One experienced traveler boards a
plane and changes immediately into a jogging suit
for international or transcontinental flights. He
changes out of the jogging suit a half hour before
arrival. (You may want to change before boarding
the plane.)

Pack Wrinkle Smart   Keep your clothes in the
plastic bags and on the hangers supplied by the
dry cleaner. As you pack garments into a suitcase,
gently roll them over once, hangers, bags, and all.
If you are taking a carry-on garment bag, keep it in
a hanging-up position as much as possible. Sleeves
of jackets will get less wrinkled if you keep tissue
paper stuffed inside them. Have the dry cleaner
fold your shirts, and pack them folded.

3 ✈ Stay in Touch

Let your family and business associates know where you are each step of the trip. Freely pass out copies of your itinerary in advance of your trip so that your family members and close work associates will know how, where, and when to reach you.

Be sure to leave the following:

- Your flight information (arrival and departure times, flight numbers, airline carrier)

- The name of each hotel and the phone number

- Facsimile machine numbers where you may be working or staying (if available)

If you make a change in your itinerary—a change in flight schedule, a hotel change—be sure to call that change back to your home and office.

Provide Emergency Information Discuss emergency procedures with your family. (If you travel a great deal, you may need to have a conversation about emergency procedures only periodically.) Make sure your spouse knows the location of key phone numbers, documents (legal and insurance, especially), and keys. Teenage children should also be told how to get in contact with you in case of emergencies at home.

Phone Home Regularly   Make a plan with your family for phone calls and then stick to your plan. (Keep time zone differences in mind!) Nothing lets your family members know that you are thinking about them—and loving them—like a phone call in which you *say so*. When you call, ask your spouse about the day and concerns. Ask your children the same kinds of questions you'd ask if you were home—questions about school, sports, play rehearsal, band practice, club meetings, and church. Tell your family about where you are— describe your hotel room, the view from your room, and the city in which you are staying. Help your loved ones picture you vividly. They'll feel more a part of your trip.

Don't rely on office helpers to convey messages to your family at home. Don't ask your family members to give messages to your secretary or boss. You'll only cause confusion and resentment.

Send Postcards   Even though your children may receive a card long after you are back home, a postcard in the mail from the place (or places) you have been will let your children know that you were thinking of them every day along the way.

"What Did You Bring Me?" If you travel extensively, you may not want to get into the habit of bringing home a gift on each trip, but periodically, you'll want to arrive home with something special for those who stay at home while you travel. You are giving more than a present; you are reassuring those at home that they are in your thoughts and heart as you travel.

4 ✈ Personalize Your Home Away from Home

After a while, all hotel rooms—no matter how expensive—begin to look alike. The wallpaper and furniture may change slightly, but you'll likely find the same pieces of furniture placed in the same general configurations room after room after room.

To personalize a hotel or motel room, try these ideas.

Put Away All of the Hotel-Provided Information Immediately Upon Your Arrival Put away the room service information, the tent cards that tell about special hotel features, the matches, the ashtrays (or extra ashtrays), the phone books, the in-city magazine, and so forth. Just getting these items out of sight will make the room look and feel less commercial.

Move into the Room Empty your suitcases (as much as you desire). Hang up your clothes. Take out your book or personal journal and put it on the nightstand next to the bed. Put the magazine you're reading on the table. Put your briefcase on the desk. You may want to set out some items on the bathroom countertop.

Rearrange the Furniture a Little to Suit You   For example, the desk may be positioned so the chair faces into the room. If you have a room with a nice view, consider turning the desk around so you're facing the outside world!

Request Only One Bed   If you're traveling alone, request only the bed you need. You'll have more space, and the room will also feel more like a bedroom.

Take Your Own Pillow   Having your own bed pillow will immediately personalize any bed. And you'll probably enjoy better sleep on the road.

Enjoy Your Own Music   Most hotel and motel rooms provide television sets. But TV may not be the best way for you to relax and unwind. You may want to take along a small compact disk player and a favorite CD or two (or a tape recorder and tapes). Give the room "your sound."

Put Out a Few Personal Icons You've Brought from Home   Here are some examples:

- A framed photograph (or two) of your family members. You may want to have Plexiglas cut for the frame to replace the regular glass.

- A small metal vase or two. Especially if you're staying more than one night in a place, indulge in some flowers to brighten the room.

- Children's toys. Before you leave, ask your children to give you something to take on the trip to remind you of them. Each child will feel honored and assured of being remembered. And you'll feel closer to loved ones at home.

5 ⌖ Pamper Your Feet

Buy only shoes that fit and are comfortable in the store. Don't expect to break in your shoes, and especially don't buy new shoes before a trip.

Flats Women travelers should choose flat-soled shoes for taking long car trips or for scurrying in and out of airports and train stations. If you need to have high heels as part of your business look, take them along in your carry-on bag, and change at the last minute before the plane lands or before you enter the meeting place.

In choosing flat shoes, you'll be doing your legs and your pocketbook a favor. Your shoes will be a lot less scuffed, and you'll have fewer broken straps and heels. You'll be a lot less likely to trip or turn an ankle, especially in walking city streets that might be unevenly paved (such as the cobbled streets of Europe).

Loose Footwear As you travel, wear footwear that you can loosen (such as sneakers, walking shoes, or sandals) or that is already loose-fitting. Feet tend to swell during long flights or car trips, and loose-fitting footwear can be a major blessing at a trip's end.

In-Flight Slippers   Some international carriers provide slippers to passengers. You may want to take along your own to wear in case the carrier on which you are traveling doesn't provide this service. Lightweight crushable shoes are best. You'll enjoy wearing these slippers in your motel room, too.

Rubber Soles   Choose shoes with rubber soles and a style of shoe that can work for you all day. Rubber soles are especially important if you are going to places where the streets and pavements are likely to be slick or where the weather is likely to include rain or snow.

Plastic Shoes   Many travelers take along thongs, flip-flops, or plastic shoes for wearing in hotel showers or at pools or for walking to and from a beach. This type of footwear is especially good to take along if you are traveling overseas where disease is frequently contracted through the skin (including the soles of feet).

An Extra Pair   Take along more than one pair of day shoes. And then alternate the shoes you wear. Give your shoes a day's rest and time to air out. The leather will last longer, and your feet will thank you.

The Classics   You'll need to take along fewer pairs of shoes if you stick to neutral colors and classic styles. Let your socks or stockings be your color-coordinating accessory.

Footwear Kit   You may want to take along a plastic bag filled with foot powder (a traveler's delight), a few bandages (for the unexpected blister), insole liners to provide extra cushioning (especially if you anticipate a great deal of walking), shoelaces, and small containers of shoe polish.

A Five-Minute Rest   At least once during the day, or at the day's end before an evening dinner appointment, take time out to take off your shoes and socks. Then lie down and elevate your feet above your heart for at least five minutes. You'll feel much more ready to go again in fresh socks and shoes.

6 ✈ Maintain Your Own Schedule

The travel industry will do its best to foist *its* schedule on you—telling you when to eat, sleep, and participate in group entertainment. Choose, instead, to maintain *your* schedule as much as possible.

Everyone seems to have a routine when it comes to battling jetlag. Be aware, however, that timelag sets in with even a two-hour time difference between arrivals and departures. You need to accommodate this difference in some way.

Reset Your Biological Clock Many travelers set their watches to arrival time immediately upon boarding a plane. They then begin mentally to live at that time.

If an in-flight meal is served at a time at which you would not normally eat (given your new time frame), turn it down. If you need to eat at regular intervals, perhaps to control blood sugar levels, take along a few emergency foods to eat when you need to.

If you would not normally watch a movie at 2:00 A.M., don't force yourself to do so. Opt for sleep instead.

Adjust Your Intake of Stimulants and Foods

A helpful tool for thousands of travelers is *The Jetlag Book* (New York: Random House, 1983). This small paperback book gives very practical suggestions for using caffeine, adjusting light and darkness, and alternating feast and famine days for jogging your body forward or backward in time. Travelers from pilots to presidents have used it. And for good reason—it works!

Set Yourself Up for Sleep

Many transoceanic flights and transcontinental flights are scheduled at night. Therefore, prepare to sleep. Don't force yourself to stay awake to eat or watch a movie.

Just before leaving for the airport, take a hot soaking bath. Get yourself as relaxed as possible. Wear very loose clothing on the flight.

Also, take along light shields for your eyes, and use them.

Let Your Seatmates Know You Are Planning to Sleep

If you have an aisle or center seat, let your seatmates know that you are planning to sleep during most of the flight. You may also want to advise the flight attendants serving you that you do not want to be awakened for a meal.

Take Along Your Own Travel Pillow

Airlines provide pillows, but they are rarely the size or shape you need for your neck or your lower back.

22*Make Business Travel Easier*

If you travel a great deal on long trips, take along
the pillow support you need.

Live in the Time Zone Upon arrival, you
may want to follow these suggestions:

- Force yourself to live in the time zone where
  you have landed. Rather than take a nap, try
  taking a brisk walk. Breathe deeply. Get
  your blood circulating. Awaken to the new
  day ahead!

- If your feet are swollen, take a shower after
  your walk, and elevate your feet for ten to
  fifteen minutes. But don't go to sleep! Keep
  the drapes wide open to let as much sun-
  shine into the room as possible. If you need
  to, get back in the shower for a few minutes
  of cool water to awaken you.

- Even if you aren't particularly hungry, eat
  something at the times when others in your
  new location are eating. Choose proteins
  over sugars.

- Go to bed at the time you normally would.
  Again, relax with a very hot bath or shower.
  Even if you do not fall asleep immediately,
  stay in bed with the room darkened.

7 ✈ Eat and Drink as a Traveler

Travel requires a steady flow of energy. That's the number one principle to remember as you choose foods and beverages.

Enjoy Airline Specialty Meals Airlines offer specialty meals for persons on low-fat, no-sugar, kosher, or low-cholesterol diets. Make sure your travel agent requests one for each of your flights, and let the flight attendant know upon boarding that you have ordered such a meal.

Specialty meals often provide a more healthy, balanced variety of foods than the regular meals—with an emphasis on salad, fish, and poultry over red meat, sweets, and sauces.

Eat Small Meals More Often Large meals tend to put the traveler into a constant state of flux between feeling bloated and feeling ravenous. Instead of eating large meals once or twice a day, choose to eat small meals more frequently.

Choose Foods Carefully Choose mild over spicy. Choose without sauce rather than with sauce. Choose fresh over canned or cooked—but only if you are in an area in which fresh foods are considered to be healthful. (In some countries, the water source for growing fruits and vegetables is contaminated; therefore, the fruits and vegetables themselves are.) Choose proteins and high-fiber carbohydrates over sugars. Your goal is to fuel yourself with sustained energy for the next three hours. Avoid energy highs and lows.

Choose Fresh Fruits and Whole Grain Snacks An apple and a few whole wheat crackers are a good minimeal to sustain energy—much more beneficial than a candy bar or piece of pie.

Drink Bottled Water Especially if you are traveling overseas, but also as a general rule of travel, choose bottled water. Make sure the cap on the bottle is sealed when you purchase it.

Drink Lots of Water Keep your system fully moisturized. If you are traveling by car, keep a large container of water with you at all times. Fill yourself up with water each time you fill the car up with gasoline. If you are facing a long flight, you may want to take a bottle of water with you or request that the flight attendant give you a carafe of water (or ongoing glasses of water).

- Choose water over coffee, tea, or carbonated beverages, which frequently have high amounts of sugar and sodium, both of which are bad news for travelers. The sugar will keep your metabolism swinging from high to low, and the sodium will cause you to retain fluids—both of which quickly lead to exhaustion. Apple juice is a good alternative to water if you feel the need for variety.

• Periodically splash water on your face. A traveler's skin tends to dry out on long flights. The best moisturizer you can use is water.

What about fluid retention? The more water you drink on a long trip, the *less* your body will feel a need to retain water.

Even if you plan to sleep on a flight, have a glass of water on your tray table to drink when you awaken.

Get Pure Water If you are traveling to an area in which you are uncertain about the water quality or the availability of bottled water, take along water purification tablets. Ask your local pharmacist for advice.

8 ✦ Take Along Emergency Foods

Don't assume that you'll always be able to find food easily.

Don't assume that you'll always be able to eat when you want to.

Don't assume that the food you are provided will be the food that you want.

You are responsible for ensuring your nutrition —whether you are going to a cosmopolitan city or a developing village.

Here are suggestions for foods to take with you:

- Small pop-top cans of tuna or chicken

- A small plastic jar of peanut butter

- Whole wheat crackers (in a container that will keep them from being crushed or broken)

- Sticks of beef jerky

- Small cans or bags of unsalted nuts, such as almonds or peanuts, or sunflower seeds

- High-energy, high-fiber granola bars (or similar items sweetened with honey or fruit juice)

These are all nutritious foods that can take the edge off hunger and also provide sustaining fuel.

Eight Ounces a Day Consider taking along eight ounces worth of emergency food for each day that you will be away. That's enough food to sustain you even in very difficult circumstances (such as finding yourself isolated in a wilderness setting through no desire of your own!).

Customs Regulations Keep in mind that fruits and vegetables, meat and milk products, and some seed products are not allowed across certain international boundaries (and especially are not allowed back into the United States once you leave). Check out the regulations before you pack for an international trip.

Nonperishables and Noncrushables Avoid taking along food items that are perishable (such as milk products) or items that can deteriorate en route and stain garments (such as fruits).

A Picnic Hamper If you are a salesperson traveling extensively by car, you may want to take along a picnic hamper and keep in it items such as cereal, fruits, and cheeses—good foods for breakfast and late afternoon snacking.

9 ✈ Learn to Accessorize

Choose two or three basic colors to travel with and then stick with them. Consider these examples:

- Navy and beige (or brown)

- Navy and gray

- Black, gray, and red

- Red, white, and blue

- Olive and khaki

- Soft brown, beige, and gray

Develop a travel wardrobe with pieces you can mix and match and layer. For example, a white turtleneck can go with a navy blazer and gray slacks (or skirt). That same navy blazer can go with a white shirt (blouse) and tie (scarf) and gray slacks (skirt). Or the turtleneck can go with a casual lightweight jacket and jeans. A more casual shirt can go with the gray slacks and a gray cardigan. And so forth.

Try to work with as few pieces as possible for a

maximum number of looks—casual to business dress.

Accessories to Create New Looks Become adept at using accessories to pull new looks together out of old pieces:

- Scarves or ties

- Belts (or long scarves that can be tied as belts)

- Jewelry (earrings, necklaces, bracelets, cuff links)

- Socks or hosiery

A Female Traveler She spent three weeks on the road with these twelve pieces, all of which fit into a hang-up garment bag:

1.–2. A black skirt and coat
3.–4. A red tweed jacket and skirt
5.–6. Two white blouses (each a different style)
   7. A black-and-white-checked jacket
   8. A black blouse
   9. A red blouse
  10. A pair of black slacks
  11. A black-and-multicolored duster (loose-fitting three-quarter-length jacket with no closures)
  12. A black sheath dinner dress

With scarves and jewelry and three pairs of shoes, she created more than two dozen looks that carried her from daytime casual to evening dressy!

A Male Traveler He went to Europe for a week with these items:

1. A dark gray suit
2. A navy blazer
3. A light gray sport jacket
4. A pair of khaki pants
5.–9. Five shirts
10. An off-white turtleneck sweater
11. A navy-and-gray cardigan-style sweater vest
12. A lightweight nylon jacket in khaki and navy

He took along four ties, an ascot, two belts, and three pairs of shoes (one pair of walking shoes). He had a different look for every occasion—from board meeting to boating.

Think versatility! It's the key for frequent business travelers when shopping for clothes.

10 ✈ Power Where and When You Need It

Don't assume that you'll be able to use your electrical appliances upon arrival, especially if you are traveling to a foreign country. Converter kits notwithstanding, plugs, sockets, and currents vary widely around the world, and the chance of your hotel having just what you need is less than fifty-fifty.

Don't assume that hotels and motels will have electrical outlets where you want them to be, either.

Power Up The best way to have the power you need and want as a traveler is to take along

- nonelectric "tools"—such as a curling iron that uses a liquid canister for fuel, battery-operated appliances, nonelectric curlers, and a nonelectric razor.

- an extension cord (especially for travel in the United States). An eight-foot-long cord is usually sufficient to get the lamp where you want it or to get the hair dryer in front of the mirror you want to use.

Choose a Simpler Style If you are a frequent traveler, and especially if you are a frequent international traveler, choose a hairstyle that doesn't require a lot of blowing, curling, or upkeep. You'll save yourself hours of fuss and frenzy if you can live with a wash-and-wear style. (You'll also be able to travel significantly lighter!)

Ask for What You Need Rather than lug around an iron, request an iron and ironing board from housekeeping upon arrival. Nearly all hotels have them for guest use. If you feel the need to take along a wrinkle buster, consider using a steamer instead of an iron. It is lighter in weight, tends to be more versatile to use in a hotel room, and cools off more quickly (for faster packing).

Buy What You Need If you are going to be in a country frequently (such as monthly trips to England or Japan), you may want to purchase the appliance you use most (such as a razor or hair dryer) in that nation. Mark it when you get home and use it only for trips to that destination point.

11 ✈ Make a To-Pack List

The best way to avoid leaving something behind is to make a list of the things you will need on a trip. Begin making your list several days in advance. Your final packing effort, then, will become a matter of gathering together the items you need.

If you travel infrequently, you may need to update this list with each trip. If you travel frequently, you may want to keep a list in the suitcase or garment bag you use most often.

In addition to your list, you may want to store certain travel items in your case on a permanent basis: personal hygiene items, shoe bags, travel hair dryer or curling iron, secretarial and medicine kits, plastic shoes, and so forth.

Minimize Fuss By thinking through the events you are facing and the clothing and business items you'll need for them, you are more likely to

- become aware of items that may need cleaning or mending in sufficient time to have them cleaned or mended.

- become aware of items that may need to be purchased or replenished (by checking your personal hygiene and sundries kits).

- become aware of items that you need to bring home from the office.

- plan your wardrobe so that you take along only what you truly need.

- use a minimal number of luggage pieces.

Don't Forget It! Below is a sample list. (Items in capital letters are major categories, which need more detailed information. HAIR ITEMS, for example, might include hair dryer, curling iron or curlers, brush, comb, shampoo, mousse, and hair spray.)

- Money/traveler's checks

- Tickets

- Credit cards

- ITEMS NEEDED FOR BUSINESS APPOINTMENTS

- Travel alarm

- Diary/journal

- Notepad

- Pens

- FUN PROJECTS
- Personal Planner
- CLOTHES: CASUAL
- CLOTHES: BUSINESS
- CLOTHES: FORMAL
- SHOES
- Umbrella
- ACCESSORIES
- Night-light
- Extension cord
- JEWELRY
- PERSONAL ICONS
- Nightwear/robe
- MEDICINES/VITAMINS
- SEWING KIT
- MANICURE SET
- PORTABLE SECRETARY (supplies)
- PERSONAL HYGIENE ITEMS (shampoo, deodorant, mouthwash, floss, toothbrush, toothpaste, razor, shaving soap, feminine hygiene items)
- HAIR ITEMS

- MISCELLANEOUS KIT (spot remover, Woolite, lint-removing brush, shoe polish, shoelaces)
- Camera and film
- Swimsuit
- Cassette or CD player/tapes or CDs

12 ✦ Take Along Your Brands

Many hotels and motels provide personal convenience items, such as soap, shampoo, and conditioner.

Rely on the availability of these items as a backup plan rather than a sure thing. In the long run, you'll probably prefer to take along your brands—brands you've come to know and trust—rather than experiment with a different brand of shampoo every night on the road.

Also, by taking along your hygiene items, you are more likely to

- take *all* of the items you need. For example, some motels provide mouthwash, but most don't. Some hotels provide toothpaste, but most don't.

- maintain the chemical balance of your skin and hair.

- feel more comfortable and confident (and probably have fewer bad hair days).

On the other hand, if you want to be adventuresome, experiment away! Keep in mind that most quality hotels have various personal care items available for guest use, even if the items aren't supplied as a routine procedure to each room. If you discover that you forgot to pack your toothbrush or that you need a fingernail file, ask the hotel to provide what you need.

Buy Travel-Size Containers An assortment of small plastic travel-size containers can be purchased for a few dollars in most large grocery stores or discount stores. Or you may want to bring home the items supplied by a hotel and trade out your brand for theirs.

Be sure to label every container. (After a while, some items can tend to look alike in a container—such as shampoo and Woolite!)

Use one container for one product for the life of that container. If you must trade out a container, make certain to wash and rinse it thoroughly before putting a different item in it. Otherwise you may find, for example, that your mouthwash produces bubbles.

Watch for Trial-Size Sales A number of manufacturers make their products available periodically in sample or trial sizes. If you see an item you use regularly on sale in these sizes, you may want to stock up.

13 ✦ Avoid Getting Overly Hungry

Most people are not aware of how much energy travel requires until they are a couple of days into a trip.

Be Aware Recognize at the outset of any journey that even though you will likely be sitting for long stretches in a car or plane, you will also be lifting, walking, and exerting yourself in ways that you don't normally. You may even discover some muscle groups you didn't know you had!

In addition, you are likely to be psyched up for the trip, which speeds up the metabolism.

Fuel Up Novice business travelers are frequently surprised at how ravenous they feel at times they don't normally eat, such as midmorning and midafternoon. Rather than stop for a snack (or "waste time" eating), they force themselves to push onward until the next main meal, by which time they are on the verge of withering from hunger. Feeling starved, they tend to overeat, which results in an after-meal lethargy. To overcome the lethargy, the travelers then nap (it's not a bad idea, but it takes more time than the midmeal snack would have taken) or throw themselves into activity, which tends to create more hunger. Very quickly, the metabolism is out of whack. Indigestion and diarrhea can result. And pretty soon, the trip becomes an endurance test rather than a fun opportunity.

The better way is to take time for those midmeal snacks. Make them as nutritious as possible. Avoid sweets and go for half a sandwich, fruit and crackers, or tea and crumpets.

Anticipate your need for energy. Take along a small container of yogurt from the breakfast buffet table, or purchase an apple and an orange as you pass a fruit stand.

Eat Rather Than Talk Some business travelers are so intent at making an impression, winning a point, or engaging in a conversation that they actually seem to forget to eat at mealtimes. Or they may be so busy answering questions that they don't get in their fair share of bites. Make certain that you eat at mealtimes.

14 ✦ Avoid Getting Overly Tired

Just as travelers have a tendency to become overly hungry, they also can become overly tired.

Most people on business trips attempt to do more in a business day than they would if they were back home at the office. Not only do they feel driven to make the trip count, but they also tend to feel responsible for being at their peak level of performance every hour of the day. That means working with an intensity and an intentionality that are physically exhausting.

Energy Drains A normal business day schedule is likely to include small breaks throughout the day to write memos, sharpen pencils, chat with a coworker, exchange casual personal comments during a business call, and perhaps even stare out a window a few moments. On the road, those moments are rarely experienced. Every minute seems filled. The result: a major energy drain.

- It takes energy to listen to another person's every word, attempting to draw out exactly what is meant.

- Committing to memory all that others say or that you desire to remember takes energy.

- Weighing every word that you say—either in conversation or in formal presentation—takes energy.

- Continually being "on"—mentally alert, quick of wit, ready to respond, flexible to change—takes energy.

To maintain such a high energy level, you need to eat right, and you need to get sufficient sleep.

Early Evenings Whenever possible, excuse yourself from evening engagements. Unless the dinner business meeting is absolutely vital, suggest that you both take a break and reconvene in the morning. (The person you are visiting probably would like a break, too.)

If you must meet someone for dinner, suggest an early dinner—six o'clock rather than eight o'clock.

Avoid late night receptions and parties.

Get to bed early and sleep as long as you can.

Naps If you have a couple of hours available in the afternoon (perhaps at a convention or conference), and especially if you know that you must be at a nighttime function, take time for a short nap. You'll feel much more refreshed for the rest of the afternoon and evening.

15 ✦ A Private Room

Insist upon having a room of your own.

Many times when people first begin to travel for a company, they will be asked to share a room with a colleague or even with a superior. Nothing can be more personally demanding and draining.

Require Your Own Space You need a place to relax, gather your thoughts, sort through the day (and your possessions), and do what you want to do when you want to do it. You need a place where you can be totally yourself.

What If? If rooming together is a matter of money, find out the difference in cost between a double room and a single room. A double room is rarely more than a third more expensive than a single room—for example, $90 for a double, $60 for a single. Two single rooms would thus cost $120. Agree to pay the difference out of your own pocket if you must. In the example cited, you'd be paying only $30, and it would be well worth it to you in the long run.

If rooming together is suggested because of another person's desire to room with you, politely decline. Suggest that you'll both be more comfortable in a space of your own. You will be!

If rooming together is mandated because the hotel has overbooked a conference or convention, politely insist. If the hotel cannot accommodate you, find another place to stay and commute to the convention.

A Matter of Respect   Don't be bashful in requesting a private room if your company requests that you travel. Privacy is a matter of respect. If you respect yourself enough to require privacy, your company will also come to respect you more.

16 ✦ A Room with a View

You may not always be able to have a room with a view, but you can always ask for one. In some cases, be prepared for a price difference (especially in New York City). Still, give yourself the option of knowing whether such a room is available and what it costs.

Room Options The frequent business traveler will want to consider these room options.

A Room at the End of the Hall You'll walk a few more steps with each trip to your room, but your room generally will be much quieter. If there's a view to be had, you're also more likely to have it. And end-of-the-hall rooms are likely to be next to fire escapes or stairs, the best place to be in the event of an emergency.

A Nonsmoker's Room If you don't smoke, request a nonsmoker's room. You'll enjoy your stay far more.

A Room with a Private Bath When traveling overseas, don't assume that your room will have a bathtub or shower connected to it, or even a sink and commode. Many mid-priced accommodations in other nations have communal shower and toilet facilities. If you want a room with a private bath, make sure you request one.

A Room on the Top Floor   If you are staying in a two- or three-story motel, request a room on the top floor. It will be quieter.

A Room on a Lower Floor   If you have a fear of being trapped in a high-rise hotel during a fire or storm, you may want to request a room on the second floor (or no higher than the third). You'll rest easier.

Peace Destroyers   Make certain that your room is *not* located

- next to an elevator.

- next to a laundry chute.

- next to an ice maker (or vending machine room).

- next to a kitchen or dining room (or directly above one).

- next to a hospitality suite (which tends to be used for parties into the wee hours of the night).

Previews   Ask the desk clerk to show you a floor plan and your room's location on it. If you don't like what you see, request a different room.

In Europe, it is not uncommon to ask to see the accommodations before agreeing to stay in a hotel or inn. If you have any question about the suitability or safety of the place in which you will be staying, ask to preview the room before registering.

17 ✈ Keep Business Out of Your Hotel Room

Regard your room at a hotel or motel as you would your personal bedroom at home—a place for relaxing, conversing informally, sleeping, and having breakfast in bed! It's not your office.

Choose a Work Space As much as possible, avoid working in your room. Take your portfolio or briefcase with you to a hotel lobby, veranda, or sitting room. Create a work space for yourself there.

In so doing, you'll be establishing for yourself a rhythm between work and rest, "on" time and "off" time. Your entire trip will have a better balance to it.

Granted, you may need to make some telephone calls from your room or read through a report. If so, plan to do your work-related tasks immediately upon arriving back in your room or just prior to leaving—and consider staying in your business clothes (or getting into your business clothes) for those calls or study sessions. That way, you'll still be able to make a complete mental shift from producing to relaxing once the work is done.

Avoid In-Room Meetings Avoid inviting others to your room for a meeting or going to another person's room for a meeting. A hotel room—with perhaps an unmade bed, towels in scattered array, and personal clothing and other objects in full view—is not an ideal business environment.

It's especially important to avoid private in-room meetings with members of the opposite sex. Nothing can break down trust or dent a good business relationship more than the appearance of moral impropriety, not to mention the temptations that actually accompany such a situation.

Take Advantage of a Suite If you absolutely must hold a meeting in your on-the-road residence, opt to stay in a place where you can get a suite. A number of suite hotels are available nationwide without extravagant prices. Hold the meeting in the "living" part of your suite, and do your relaxing in the "bedroom" area. Keep the door between the two areas closed.

18 ✦ Keep Your Clothes Clean

Nothing can fray the nerves quite as much as wondering whether your garments are going to make it back from the dry cleaners before your flight takes off!

Immediately upon your return home from a business trip, have your business clothes dry-cleaned or washed and your shoes polished. Check your supplies of stored-in-the-case sundries and personal hygiene items, and replenish them.

If any item has spilled in your case, clean the inside thoroughly. It's a good idea to brush clean or vacuum your case periodically.

On-the-Road Cleaning Take along spot remover with you as you travel. Very small bottles are available. You might also want to take along a couple of packets of dry Woolite or other cold-water washing powder (or perhaps a small plastic container of liquid soap). That way, if your stay on the road is extended or you find that you haven't brought along enough underwear or hosiery for the trip, do a little hand laundry along the way.

Be wary of drying your clothes on radiators or putting them too close to heating devices in a room. If items are still damp at the time you need to depart from your room, wrap them in a plastic hotel laundry bag, and put the bag in an area of your case where possible seepage won't damage other garments.

Pay a hotel laundry service to wash or dry-clean major items, such as shirts or blouses. If an item needs special handling, make certain you communicate that to the hotel valet. If you have any doubt as to whether the valet understands the need for special handling of your suede, silk, or sequined fabrics, wait until you get home to have them cleaned.

Dirty Clothes Pack a couple of extra plastic bags or use the plastic bags that hotels provide for laundry to keep your dirty clothes segregated from your clean garments.

Let your shoes and garments air out thoroughly before repacking them.

You may want to consider placing a small sachet of your favorite scent in your suitcase or a small sachet or scented card in a shoe protector bag (one for each shoe). The scented advertisement cards sent out in direct-mail or invoice packets—or the scented strips in magazines—also are good on-the-road deodorizers for your garments and shoes. Don't release the scent until you are ready to insert the piece of paper into your case.

19 ✦ Keep Your Clothes in Good Repair

In addition to keeping your clothes clean and ready to travel, you'll want to keep them in good repair.

At Home Immediately upon returning home from a trip,

- check your clothing carefully for rips, tears, loose buttons, or missing closures (snaps, hooks and eyes), and fix any problem areas, even before you clean the garments.

- check your shoes. Is it time for new heels or new heel tips? New soles? Other types of repair or reinforcement?

- check your luggage. Has it been damaged during the trip? If so, now is the time to have it repaired or restitched.

Travel is hard on clothing. You generally will walk more and call upon your clothing to move (bend, stretch, turn, or crush) in ways it doesn't normally move. Choose sturdy fabrics for travel and whenever possible, fabrics that have some give to them (such as knits). Avoid straight lines to give yourself more bending room.

Before a trip, check seams to make sure they are stitched tightly, and check buttons and closures to make sure they are firmly attached.

On-the-Road Repairs   Take a small sewing kit with you. A couple of needles, a few safety pins, a couple of miniature spools of thread, an extra button, and an extra snap set and hook and eye closure can all fit nicely into a recycled prescription bottle.

If you find yourself on the road and need repairs to a garment that you are unable to make (owing to lack of time or access to a sewing kit), ask the hotel's valet to help you.

Extra Laces   One of the most valuable items you can remember to take on a trip is an extra pair of shoelaces. Few things are as disconcerting as coping with broken laces en route to an important meeting.

20 ✦ Avoid Alcohol

Alcohol affords many more downfalls than benefits to both the body and the mind of the traveler. Consider it "off limits" if you want to get the most out of a trip.

Diminished Abilities Drinking diminishes abilities to respond quickly to an emergency or a change. And since travel involves a nearly continual flow of changes and an ongoing stream of unfamiliar sights and experiences, you'll want to avoid drinking if you want to engage fully in the experience of your trip. Alcohol lowers awareness and increases response time, a deadly or dangerous combination when you're driving or walking—especially if the streets and byways are unfamiliar. In a strange environment, you'll want to keep all your wits about you!

Relaxed Senses Many people drink to help them relax and be more sociable. In business situations, however, it pays to keep your mind completely clear and your senses continually on the alert. You're far more likely to damage your reputation by drinking too much than by not drinking at all. Choose fruit juice or an exotic herbal tea instead.

Travelers frequently drink to help them relax and sleep while on a plane, bus, or train. Find another means of relaxing. You'll arrive at your destination far more alert and ready for action. Your response time in case of any kind of travel emergency will also be quicker.

Coming Unwound Travelers often drink to help them unwind at the end of a day. Go for a walk, get a massage, take a swim in the hotel pool, or soak in a hot tub instead. Your body will thank you.

Body Harm Alcohol dries the skin, which travel already tends to do, given the lack of humidity in most public environments (especially planes and office buildings). Your skin is the largest organ of your body. When it's dry, it's tired. When it's tired, you are, too.

Alcohol also has a high sugar content, which can lead to metabolic swings.

Foreign "Punch" Be especially wary of alcoholic beverages in foreign lands. They are often suggested as a substitute for impure water. The fact is, alcoholic beverages in other countries often have a higher alcohol proof or a different "punch" from that of American-manufactured beverages. They can put you under the table far faster and with much more severe "morning after" symptoms.

All in all, don't drink and travel. You'll get more out of your trip.

21 ✦ Get Sufficient Exercise

No Excuses *Exercise* is probably the last word you want to hear by the end of your third day on the road.

"I'm Beat" The fact is, when you are tired, it's usually *not* because of exercise. The exhaustion you begin to feel after several days on the road is rooted in stress, a change in time zones and daily routine, and a lack of sleep. Exercise can actually help you feel more energy physically. It can also help you sleep better, improve your circulation, even out your metabolism in an unfamiliar environment, and help give you a clearer mind and sharper senses.

"I'm Getting More Exercise Than I Do at Home" This statement also tends to be false, depending, of course, on how much you normally exercise. What *does* happen is that you use muscles you may not normally use—muscles required to lift and tote and reach. The walking required by travel, however, rarely raises the heart rate to an aerobic level. You're moving more but not necessarily giving your heart and lungs a workout.

"When Would I Ever Find the Time to Exercise?"
You won't find the time. You'll have to make it. Set
apart a half hour every day you are on the road for
exercise. And stick to your commitment.

The Prime Travel Exercise   The one exercise you can do just about anywhere in the world is
to walk. Ask your hotel concierge (or motel clerk)
to map out a safe route for you or to direct you to a
nearby mall, school, or park track. Walking in the
early morning is a great way to begin a day in a
new city. You'll get a good feel for your where-
abouts, the people of the city, and the early morning customs. You'll feel more in sync with the place
where you will be doing business temporarily.

Furthermore, you don't need to take any special
equipment or clothing with you to walk. And you
can walk in just about any climate or location. Walk
briskly. Take in the sights along the way.

Stairs   If the weather is inclement or the neighborhood in which you are staying isn't conducive
to a brisk morning walk, try the hotel stairwell as a
place to exercise. Stair climbing provides a hearty
workout.

Hotel Spas   Many hotels and motels provide
pools, exercise rooms, or weight-training rooms.
Take advantage of them. One of the best times to
avail yourself of these facilities is during the regular dinner hour. The pool or exercise room is
nearly always less crowded at this time. Go for an

early light dinner, and then after a little break, hit the exercise area. Follow your workout with a hot shower and you'll be primed for a relaxing evening and a good night's sleep.

Isometric Exercises Even as you sit on a plane or relax in a hotel room, try isometric exercises. On long flights, get up and walk the aisles a little to improve your circulation.

22 ✈ Work with a Reliable Travel Agent

Don't hip hop from one travel agent to the next. Find one on whom you can rely, and cultivate a relationship with that person.

Let the agent know that you're looking for a long-term business relationship. As the person gives you good advice and great bargains, you'll give the agent your consistent, loyal business. Such a relationship is something an agent will usually work hard to maintain.

Look for an agent who has a twenty-four-hour hot line. If you are stranded someplace, it's likely going to be on a weekend or after hours! It's nice to know you can call for help.

Give Your Agent Room to Find the Best Deal Let your travel agent know where you need to go and when you need to be there, and then be clear about how flexible you can be. Tell your agent whether you can leave a day earlier or stay a day later (for a reduced fare). Let the person know if the date of your meeting is flexible. Are you willing to fly with any carrier? Are you willing to leave early in the morning or arrive late at night or fly all night?

Ask Your Agent for Tips Most travel agents are fellow business travelers. They are out on the road themselves. When they aren't, they generally are reading about travel and about things to do and see in various cities around the world. Ask your travel agent for suggestions. Does he have a favorite business hotel in Paris? Does she have a favorite restaurant in Atlanta? Has she heard about a good place to shop in Minneapolis? What would he do if he had a half day free in Tokyo?

Establish a Profile Your travel agent should have on file pertinent information related to you as a traveler: what type of car you like to rent, whether you prefer an aisle or a window seat, and whether convenience or price is more important to you. Your travel agent should also know what type of hotel room you prefer: smoking preference, general location in the building, and so forth.

Double-Check Your Reservations A couple of hours before (or the evening before) your departure time, call the airline to make sure your flight is still on schedule. If you are headed for a convention, you may also want to call to confirm your hotel reservations. Make sure that you have been confirmed for a late arrival if you are arriving after normal business hours.

Keep Confirmation Numbers Handy
When making a reservation with an airline, car rental agency, or hotel, you generally are given a

confirmation number. Keep the numbers with your trip itinerary.

Bear in mind always that the best travel deals are the best deals for you. Each person is different. The only way your travel agent can personalize a trip to your liking is for you to provide as much information as possible about yourself and your travel likes and dislikes.

23 ✦ Ask for More Light

Many motel and hotel rooms feel like a twilight zone. A little dull in color and decor. And usually a lot dull when it comes to light.

Furthermore, many motel and hotel rooms have been designed so that windows—which might otherwise be an excellent source of light—provide a better look *into* your room than out of it. (Nearly every traveler has had the experience of pulling open the drapes only to stare into the eyes of a passerby on a public walkway. Hotel windows frequently provide a great view of a parking lot or a look into a window across a narrow alleyway.)

What are you to do?

Lights All Over   Turn on the lights. Turn on every available light in your room. Reposition lights for an even flow of light throughout the whole room. And if the room still seems dull to you, request more light.

More Watts   First check the light bulb wattage presently in the lamps in your room. And then call down to the housekeeping desk and request higher wattage light bulbs for every lamp in your room. If they don't have such bulbs, or if you still want more light, request an additional lamp.

You need to be prepared, of course, for the possibility that with more light, you are going to see your room a little differently. The furniture and upholstery may be a little shabbier than you had thought, the carpet or wallpaper a little more soiled or in need of repair.

Still, light does wonders for your morale in a new place. It casts a brighter glow on your reason for being there, your likelihood of success, and your feelings about the city as a whole. In requesting more light, you are also enhancing your feelings of being able to take charge of a situation in a new environment.

A Night-Light, Too   If you want to be able to get up in the middle of the night without stumbling and without turning on a major light (which tends to disrupt your sleeping pattern), you may want to take along a small night-light as you travel. There's something comforting about having a little light to help you orient yourself when you awaken to find yourself in a strange room in a strange city.

24 ✦ Personal Fun

Nobody can work twenty-four hours a day. At least, not for very many days in a row!

A little diversion on a business trip is a good thing.

Favorite Things Take along some things that you can do for fun as you fly, relax in your hotel room, or eat your breakfast for one in a hotel coffee shop. It might be

- a novel.

- a magazine (which you may want to pick up in a hotel or air terminal shop).

- a small piece of needlework (embroidery, needlepoint, lace making).

- a puzzle book.

- an inspirational book (or Bible).

- an electronic game (lots of choices—from chess to Game Boy cartridges!).

Give yourself a few minutes every day for play. You'll benefit from the mental break, and you'll also feel as if your life is a little more balanced.

Even on the Road   If you are a big video fan, check out the offerings made available for in-room viewing. Plan for a time when you can curl up and watch a movie—not only because it's readily available but also because it's fun for you. The same goes for big-screen viewing. Check out the local listings. If you've been working night and day for several days, give yourself a night off to go to the movies.

If golf or tennis is your sport, take your clubs or racket along. You never know when you might run into a business colleague who is also a golf or tennis fanatic.

If you are a big sports fan, check the local team action. You may even find that your team is visiting the city in which you are staying!

Enjoy!   The point is this: do a little on the road of what you would normally do at home just for fun. In so doing, you'll begin to establish a seamless consistency between being on the road and being at home. When that happens, you'll find yourself dreading travel less.

25 ✈ Sampling What the New Place Offers

In exploring a city, you'll learn a little about what it means for your colleagues, clients, or vendors to live and work there full-time. You'll develop more empathy with them.

Read the Local Newspaper Become familiar with the issues and personalities. Has a local team experienced a major victory (or defeat)? Is the city facing a major bond issue? Is there a strike going on? Is a major crime investigation or trial under way? The folks around the business table will be talking about it; you might as well know what's going on.

Experience the Local Specialties It might be local theater (or in the case of New York City, the finest theater smorgasbord in America). It might be a local symphony concert, ballet, or opera. It might be a local amusement park or other tourist attraction.

The local specialties, of course, include favorite restaurants. They include the primo shopping area or a place related to the industry in the area (such as a wharf or factory that is open to visitors).

Ask for Suggestions   Ask your travel agent, the hotel concierge, your cabdriver, or your business colleagues in the city: "What's the best way to have a couple of hours of fun in this area?" Just about anybody you ask will gladly give you a suggestion or two. If a cultural performance, sporting event, or tourist attraction is suggested, ask the hotel concierge to help you get tickets.

Also ask, "What's the local food specialty?" Nearly every city has one: Boston has its chowder, Baltimore its crab cakes, New Orleans its gumbo, Kansas City its steaks, Philadelphia its cheese steak sandwiches, and so forth. Try out the local fare.

If you are in a restaurant, ask the waiter, "What do you think are the two best dishes this chef prepares?" You may as well experience the house specialties (which may or may not be the "chef's suggestions" for the day).

Take Overview Tours   Sometimes the best way to initially become familiar with a new city is to take a tour of it. Ask a cabdriver to show you the city sights. Agree on a price and time frame in advance, and go over what the driver is going to show you. Or if you have rented a car, ask a hotel concierge, desk clerk, or business colleague in the city to map out a self-guided tour route for you. In a city with excellent transportation systems, such as the double-decked buses and the "tubes" in London or the Metro in Paris, purchase a multiple-fare pass and explore!

Shop Overseas Perhaps more so overseas than in the United States, some places are frequently known for their particular wares: lacquer boxes or nesting dolls in Moscow, lace in Brussels, woolen goods and crystal in Dublin, opals in Sydney, electronics in Hong Kong, made-to-order suits in Taiwan. Ask hotel personnel or your business colleagues for suggestions about where you might find good bargains on local specialties. Be a little suspicious, however, if someone offers to take you to a certain store or readily offers you a business card of a "cousin" who specializes in just what you need.

26 ✈ Having the Right Luggage

The real two-piece business suit is likely to be a garment bag and a carry-on bag!

Your luggage is important. Choose luggage with four qualities in mind.

First, Your Luggage Needs to Stand Up to Travel Hard-sided luggage usually survives extensive travel best. If you choose soft-sided luggage, go for leather or for fabrics that are sturdy (very heavy weave). In purchasing luggage, look for sturdy frames, tightly sewn seams and reinforcements, tight closures, reinforced edges and corners, and a comfortable carrying handle. Check out straps and handles to make certain they are attached securely.

Second, Your Luggage Needs to be Easy to Manipulate and Move Choose two smaller pieces rather than one large piece for business travel. That way, you can carry them onto your plane, maneuver your way through crowds with ease, and all the while distribute the weight for less physical stress.

If you choose luggage that you can carry over-the-shoulder style, make sure the straps are padded, are long enough, and can be stored or tightened so they don't snag, rip, or become tangled up with other items if the bag is checked.

Many styles of luggage now come equipped with wheels and handles. Check them out! Literally. Try pulling them across the store. The wheels must be retractable, wide, and fixed. The handle—which must also be retractable—should be long enough so that you don't need to bend over to pull the suitcase.

You may want to explore the possibility of taking a portable luggage carrier with you. These mini-cart devices usually fold up and can be taken onto a plane as carry-on luggage. Sometimes, however, they can be as cumbersome or heavy as a piece of luggage.

Third, Your Luggage Needs to Hold What You Are Taking Let your particular travel needs and style dictate the type of luggage you choose. Duffel bags may look great and be highly versatile, but they don't do much to keep a packed business suit from wrinkling. A suitcase with lots of pockets may be one you'd like rather than a suitcase with one large compartment.

As you examine a piece of luggage, imagine how you will pack it. Where will various items go? How accessible will the items be en route or upon arrival? How much repacking will you need to do on a daily basis?

Fourth, Your Luggage Sends a Signal About Your Particular Style   Choose understated luggage in solid colors or subtle tweeds. Keep in mind that your luggage appears as an accessory to those who observe you, including colleagues who pick you up from an airport or hotel, or who travel with you. A simple rule of style: don't let your luggage detract from *you*.

27 ✈ Having the Right Gear

In addition to your luggage—your foremost gear as a traveler—you'll find these items to be of great value.

Swiss Army Knife Choose one that has a can opener, bottle opener, fingernail file, screwdriver head, and a small pair of scissors in addition to a couple of knife blades. This is one area worth getting top-of-the-line gear with as many accessories as you think you may use.

Oversize Wallet Find a large wallet folder that is big enough to hold your passport, tickets, itinerary, money, credit cards, and perhaps even a map. Keep it in your carry-on bag, and once out of a plane, don't take your hands off your bag! (The folder will be safer there than in one of your pockets or in a purse.)

Zippered Wallet This simple slim-line carrier is designed primarily for currency. You may prefer a model that has more than one interior pocket, so you can carry various types of currency (if you are traveling to multiple nations) or so you can carry receipts in one side of the wallet and cash in the other. Your cash will be more secure with the zipper. You may want to tuck this into the oversize wallet or travel folder described above if you have room.

Fold-Up Umbrella   You never know when it's going to rain, even in an otherwise arid place.

Extra Suitcase   Take along a nylon bag (one with handles that zippers shut) that folds flat and takes up virtually no room in your suitcase. That way, if you find special buys or souvenirs along the way, or if you need to bring back more business documents than you had originally anticipated, you'll have an extra bag that you can load and carry as hand luggage (or even check).

Key-Chain Flashlight   Take along a small flashlight—the kind that might double as a key chain—to help you find something in your case or purse during a night flight, find the right key for the car, open the hotel room door at the end of a dimly lit hall, read a menu in a dimly lit restaurant, or read a map.

28 ✦ Arriving Intact

One of a traveler's worst nightmares is the possibility of arriving at the destination without the luggage.

Here are some tips to ensure that you and your possessions stay together.

Carry Your Bags with You Whenever possible, carry all of your luggage with you on the plane. If you are traveling only overnight or for two or three days, you can probably manage this with little effort. If you can avoid checking your luggage, you will ensure yourself of having everything you need as you travel, and your luggage will receive less damage. You'll also save yourself lots of time in baggage claim areas of airports.

Make Sure All of Your Luggage Is Tagged with a Permanent Identification Card Clearly Providing Your Name and Address For security purposes, you may want to purchase tags that have fold-over flaps so that your name and address aren't read easily.

Put an Identification Tag or Sticker on the Inside of Your Luggage Provide your name, your permanent phone number, and your travel address. You may also want to tuck a copy of your itinerary in each case.

Lock Your Luggage Although expert baggage thieves are able to pick such locks easily, locking your bags acts as a deterrent to a thief who may be in a hurry.

Use a Wide Colorful Strapping Belt to Secure Your Case Even Further Wrap the strap around your case and through the carrying handle, a method that in many instances will also cover the lock on the suitcase. Not only will such a strap keep your case more secure (and help you avoid the embarrassment of seeing your possessions strewn over a baggage turntable), but it will make your suitcase easier to identify.

Make Certain That You Give Your Bags Only to Authorized Airline Personnel for Check-In Purposes Don't let your bags out of your sight at a hotel. Go with your luggage to your hotel room.

Do All Your Packing at Home Avoid getting into your cases at an airline terminal. Potential thieves will be more tempted to steal a bag they *know* has valuables in it.

Never Put Cash, Jewelry, Cashier's Checks, Bonds, Furs, or Other Valuable Items in Suitcases That You Are Going to Check Carry these items on your person, or put them in carry-on luggage that you will have with you at all times.

Double-Check the Destination Tags That the Airline Personnel Put on Your Checked Luggage Learn the codes for various airports (DFW for Dallas-Fort Worth, LAX for Los Angeles, for example). Know what the code is supposed to be for your destination, and make certain that you see that abbreviation on your bags before you leave them at the check-in point. Remove used tags at the end of each segment of your trip to avoid confusion.

Be in the Baggage Claim Area When Your Bags Arrive Be present to claim your luggage as soon as it comes off the baggage conveyor belts.

29 ✦ Keep Your Expense Account Current

Take time each day to sort through your expenses and record them on a master list or form (either one of your creation or one provided by your firm).

Correct Accounts Make sure the date and amount are printed clearly on each receipt. If there's a question about what the receipt is for, make a note on it, including the names of persons you may have included in entertainment, restaurant, or other similar charges. You might also want to make a notation about what you discussed.

If you don't have a receipt for an expenditure, put the cash amount on a separate slip of paper, date it, and indicate the nature of the expense and the place of purchase.

Complete Accounts In taking a few minutes to record your expenses each day,

- you are much more likely to recall all of your expenses.

- you will have an up-to-date feel for how much money you are spending (and whether

you are within the amounts budgeted for
your trip).

• you will have your records in order at the
trip's end for a speedier filing (and usually a
speedier reimbursement) of expenses.

• you will be able to use your expense account
as something of a log of your trip, a re-
minder of follow-up tasks or correspondence
that may be warranted.

Keep all of your receipts together and in some
sense of order by date. They'll be easier to sort
through later.

As You Spend . . . Put your receipts in one
place rather than stuff one into a pocket, another
into a wallet, and still others into a briefcase. Get
into the habit of asking for receipts at parking ga-
rages and for individual checks at restaurants.

30 ✈ Seek Out a Time of Peace

Travel is noise intensive, people intensive, visually intensive, and aroma intensive. It all adds up to exhaustion.

Make certain that you find a time each day to

- be quiet. Turn off the TV in your hotel room or the radio in the rental car.

- be alone. Get away from the crowds, your colleagues, and even your traveling companion.

- be in a place of beauty. It may be a nearby park or garden. It may be an atrium or a veranda of the hotel where you are staying. Soak in a little of nature's wonder. Get away from the sounds of traffic and the smell of diesel exhaust, away from the sounds of machinery and the smell of street vendor hot dogs. Get away from the clutter of omnipresent billboards and commercial displays. Give your eyes, ears, and nose a rest.

Create Your Own Space You may need to create such a spa for yourself. If so, try purchasing some flowers at a roadside flower stand, or pick them up from a street vendor or at a hotel shop. Buy a couple of votive or dinner candles. Fill a bathtub with scented bubbles. Light the candles, turn off the lights, take the bouquet to a spot where the candles can illuminate them, and soak awhile.

Take a Fifteen-Minute Vacation You might also create this space in your imagination. Close your eyes and daydream for a few minutes of a far-distant place that is beautiful and quiet and filled with natural aroma. For example, envision yourself walking along a pristine beach and hearing only the lapping of waves, smelling only the saltiness of the spraying surf. Or imagine yourself watching the rise of a full moon from a balcony overlooking the ocean, again hearing the surf; this time, breathe in deeply the aroma of the jasmine intertwined with the latticework on your imaginary balcony. In sum, take a vacation from work.

Enjoy the Benefits of Such a Break Taking a break from the hustle and bustle of travel will do three things for you:

1. It will give you a time to restore your sense of identity and personhood. You'll feel less like a number in the rush of the masses.

2. It will allow you to collect your thoughts, process the day's events, draw conclusions, regroup your emotions, and pull yourself together before facing the next appointment on your schedule.

3. It will allow you time away from "required"

thinking to be creative. Let your imagination soar. Completely leave the work schedule and tasks behind, and think about something totally off the wall. You'll be able to return to your schedule and agenda with a much fresher mind-set.

Give yourself the gift of peace in the midst of chaos. You'll be better equipped to cope with the demands of travel.

31 ✈ Take Your Business Gear

Be sure to pack all the business gear you'll need on your trip.

Don't Forget the Batteries Take your pocket calculator, including an extra set of batteries. Don't rely on equipment at your destination point. Go prepared.

If you are doing interviews or will need to tape-record a meeting, take along a spare recorder and, again, extra batteries. Be sure to take along more tapes than you think you will use.

If you are doing work that will require your notebook computer, take it along. Don't forget the battery pack. If you are certain that a computer is available for your use at your destination point, double-check its make and model, and take your data diskettes.

If you suspect that you will need to photograph any part of the trip—to document information, create a record of the meeting or event, or take photographs of the innovation you have been sent to explore—be sure to take along your camera and all necessary lenses. Take extra film and batteries, too.

Renting Equipment In some cases—such as making major presentations with overhead projectors, film projectors, and/or video projectors or videotaping an event—you may need to rent equipment in the city to which you are traveling. Make certain that you rent from a reputable dealer or supplier who will guarantee the equipment and, if possible, provide a technician or operator. It's a good idea to arrive a few hours before the meeting, or even the day before, to rehearse with the equipment. A rehearsal makes your presentation flow more smoothly and ensures that the equipment is in good working order.

Never Assume the Availability of Equipment

Never assume that another person is going to cover the equipment needs for a meeting, interview, or sales presentation. Don't even assume the availability of a typewriter, copy machine, or fax machine. Rather, assume that nothing will be provided for you, not even a notepad or pen. That way, you'll always be prepared.

32 ✈ Take Along Vital Reference Materials

Certain reference materials and travel information are vital to the seasoned business traveler.

Schedules If you regularly travel by plane, pick up an airline schedule for the carrier you usually fly. Or subscribe to *OAG Desktop Flight Guide* (published every two weeks by OAG Official Airline Guide, 2000 Clearwater Drive, Oak Brook, Illinois 60521). That way, should you need to adjust your itinerary or catch a later flight, you'll have the information you need at your fingertips. (Prodigy, CompuServe, and other online computer services, also provide thorough travel information. You may be able to plug into these systems on the road, using your laptop computer.)

The same goes for train or bus schedules. Having a copy of a master schedule can give you more flexibility as you travel and help you make mid-course adjustments easily and quickly.

In your address book, you may want to list the toll-free numbers for the services you regularly use:

- Airlines (and include your air-mileage account numbers, too)

- Rental car companies

- Major hotel chains

Road Atlas   If your business travel is mostly by car, obtain a good road atlas and comprehensive city maps for the cities in which you regularly conduct business.

Personal Planner Aids   Many personal planning systems (such as Filofax, Daytimer, Rolodex, and Dayrunner systems) have maps that provide information about

- time zones.

- area codes.

- city maps (for the largest cities in America or Europe).

Make certain that you adjust your thinking about time zones during daylight savings time months.

City Maps   Ask your hotel or rental car agency to provide you with a map for a city that is new to you. And if you plan to use a subway, get a copy of the city's mass transit map. Have the concierge or a knowledgeable hotel clerk help you map routes to your appointments.

Calling Card Don't forget your international calling card (a wallet card issued by your long-distance service), a very handy piece of plastic for those who travel overseas. Make certain that you have international phone codes with you for every nation you plan to visit on your itinerary.

33 ✈ Travel Without Valuables

The general rule about traveling with valuables can be expressed in one word: *don't!*

If, however, you feel that you must travel with certain valuable items,

- use the hotel safety deposit boxes for cameras, electronic gear, jewelry, and extra cash or traveler's checks.

- always carry valuable items on your person or in your carry-on luggage as opposed to putting them in suitcases that you are checking.

- be discreet in your use of valuables. Don't flaunt your expensive items or leave them lying in open view where they might tempt pickpockets or hotel workers.

Money One valuable you probably can't leave at home is money. Whenever possible, use traveler's checks, which can be reimbursed should you lose them or have them stolen. Traveler's checks are especially important for long trips or overseas trips.

In carrying cash, you'll find a zippered wallet or purse more secure than one without a zipper.

Rather than carry two hundred-dollar bills, carry ten twenty-dollar bills, and keep seven of them in a place other than your wallet (such as your travel folder, purse, or traveler's check wallet).

Again, be discreet in handling money. Don't flash a large roll of bills. The person most likely to be impressed is a thief. Be cautious in using automatic teller machines that allow you to access cash with a major credit card.

Cards   Be as private and discreet as possible in your use of calling cards. Don't let others watch you punch in personal identification codes or overhear you giving your personal identification number to a telephone operator. (You could find hundreds of dollars worth of long-distance calls on your next bill. Phone thieves regularly attempt to overhear or pick up card numbers as they cruise airport telephone stations.)

Watch closely the way in which a clerk handles your credit card. Always ask for any carbon impressions. Since most transaction devices are located in view of customers (except in restaurants), question the actions of a clerk who attempts to leave your sight with your card or write your card number on a separate piece of paper. Make certain that the clerk does not make *two* impressions with your card, and that any "mistakes" be ripped up in your presence or be given to you.

Passport and Tickets   Keep your passport and travel tickets with you at all times. In some overseas hotels, you will be required to surrender your passport as a part of the check-in procedure. At all other times, carry your passport with you, and guard it carefully.

34 ✈ Currency Exchanges

If you are making a trip to another country, plan in advance to arrive in that nation with the foreign currency that you will need in the form of cash or traveler's checks. Have on hand at least enough cash for a meal, a few phone calls, and a cab ride into town.

You can usually get foreign currency from the international department of a major bank. (In some cases, you may need to order the money several days or a week in advance.) If you are unable to order currency in advance, try to exchange currency at the international terminal before your departure. You'll usually get better rates in the United States *before you leave* than you will get upon arrival in another nation.

Stay Aware of Exchange Rates Become adept at converting currency; stay aware of exchange rates on a daily basis. Above all, make certain that you are working the mathematical equations in the right way. Pity the traveler who gets things backward! (The belt that costs £20 with a 2.5 exchange rate to the U.S. dollar is not a bargain at $8; rather, it's a fairly expensive belt costing $50!)

Always look for the U.S. dollar exchange rate as opposed to other dollars (Canadian and Australian, among others).

Calculation Lag You will be able to use your major credit cards in many places overseas, but the currency amount nearly always will be calculated at the time the transaction is posted, not at the time of your purchase. Keep a running record for yourself as to the estimated amounts you have charged; in posting your expense account, however, recognize that they will not necessarily be the actual amounts. You'll need to double-check your expenses when your credit card bills are processed.

Other Precautions Many foreign clerks, hotels, and shop owners will exchange money on site but usually at the highest possible exchange rate. Whenever possible, exchange currency at a bank, an American Express office, or an international exchange.

Be aware that

- exchange rates vary, according to whether you are exchanging cash or traveler's checks or using charge accounts. The rate for traveler's checks is usually the most advantageous.

- you will be charged a transaction fee each time you exchange money; rather than exchange only a few dollars at a time, exchange what you think you will need in a country.

- you cannot exchange coins.

Just prior to leaving a nation, convert as much of your change as possible into paper currency, and spend the rest on sundries.

Your Own Cash Pool If you travel extensively overseas, you are likely to build up something of a "bank" of your own in international currencies. Consider keeping money from different nations in separate envelopes in your desk at work or home. Label the envelopes clearly. Include any coins you may have brought home. You'll have a head start in preparing for your next trip.

35 ✈ Getting to the Right Address

Keep your address book current. And make certain that you have included in it all the names and numbers you are likely to need. There's nothing quite as frustrating as not having the number you need to call and not remembering the middle initial of the Smith you need to reach.

You may find it helpful to transfer business card information into a more permanent address book (or address book section of a personal planning system) as soon as possible after receiving a person's card. That way, you'll avoid what sometimes becomes a frantic search through pockets for a missing business card.

Take along a few first-class stamps, including a few first-class postcard stamps. You'll find it easier to send your children or spouse a card from your faraway place of business.

Overseas If you are traveling overseas, stamps can be difficult to come by. In some countries, they are sold only at a post office. Your hotel concierge or desk clerk may be able to help you.

Overnight Delivery Make certain that you take your account numbers with you if you plan to use an overnight delivery service while you are on the road.

Get It in Writing In receiving directions or address information from another person, ask the person to write the address for you. Have paper and pen ready for that purpose. That way, you can hand the piece of paper directly to a cabdriver (or to the concierge who is helping you find the place on your map). This is an especially practical tip if you travel in foreign countries or in an area where you have difficulty understanding a regional dialect!

36 ✈ A Portable Secretary

You'll find it valuable to take along a little portable secretary of supplies commonly needed on a business trip. A number of these kits are available on the market, or you can create your own by collecting these items and putting them in a resealable plastic bag or a fabric pouch:

- A small pair of scissors (airline regulations stipulate that scissors you carry onto a plane cannot have blades longer than two inches)

- Scotch tape or other type of tape

- A ministapler and extra staples

- Assorted rubber bands

- Paper clips

- Pens—if you take an ink pen, make sure to take extra ink cartridges

- Pencils (if you need them) and a small pencil sharpener

You may also want to consider taking some Post-it Notes, correction fluid, and extra markers or grease pencils (that may be needed for overhead transparency presentations or photography work).

Computer Supplies If you are traveling with your computer, you may want to take along an extra battery pack (or a rechargeable unit) and extra formatted diskettes. Consider taking a backup copy of the word processing or spreadsheet program that you use regularly.

In-Transit Services Some airports now have in-transit secretarial service outlets—computers, facsimile machines, stationery and supplies, and even secretarial assistance. Outlets for sending fax messages are also becoming more common. The lounges offered to members of airline clubs also provide secretarial support services in nearly all cases.

Beware of Ink You will probably find it wise to leave your fountain pen at home. A number of fountain pens do not work well at high altitudes (that is, on planes). They also tend to leak in unpressurized environments (that is, all over your garments in checked luggage). Dealing with liquid ink or ink cartridges with liquid ink can be messy on the road.

Supplies When You Need Them By taking along a personal secretary of this type, you'll have supplies where and when you need them. Such items come in especially handy if you need to crash together a revision or a presentation in your hotel room or en route to a meeting.

37 ✈ Wash Your Hands

The best way to stay healthy on a trip is actually a very easy way: wash your hands often.

The primary way that many diseases are transmitted is through the mouth, and most viral and bacterial diseases reach the mouth by means of the hand. In other words, you touch something crawling with germs and then you touch your lips, or you touch something (including food) that you then put into your mouth.

Most people inadvertently touch their mouths far more than they realize. They also touch germ-laden surfaces far more than they want to think about—from handles and handrails to menus and machine knobs.

Wash Carry a bar of soap with you in a small plastic bag. If soap isn't available in the rest room you are using, you'll have your own supply. (When traveling overseas, never count on the availability of soap in any public facility.)

Use warm water.

Wash your hands from above the wrist downward. Don't just wash the tips of your fingers.

Dry Dry your hands thoroughly, but avoid using cloth towels that are made available for general public use. Use paper towels or electric dryers instead, or simply let your hands air dry.

Use the paper towel you have used to dry your hands to open the rest room door, or cover your hand with your skirt or jacket to open the door. (Many people leave a rest room with as many germs on their hands as when they walked in!)

Wash Again Always wash your hands before eating (even a snack), and always wash your hands after using the toilet.

Immediately upon arriving in your hotel room, wash your hands, even before you begin to unpack.

After any public meeting or any situation in which you have been asked to shake hands with a number of people, excuse yourself and wash your hands.

Obviously, hand washing can become an obsessive or compulsive behavior. That isn't at all what's being recommended here. What is being suggested is that you safeguard your health as much as possible on the road.

38 ✦ Prepare to Tip

Never consider that you are traveling alone.

Many people are required not only to make your trip possible but also to make your trip easier. Those who make your trip possible tend to be those you pay—in the form of tickets, lodging, and meals. Those who make your trip easier are people you should plan to tip.

Carry about twenty to thirty dollars in one-dollar bills, and be willing to spend them.

Luggage Don't waste your energy carrying heavy luggage through airports or hotels. Tip the porter or bellcap who is available to do that work for you. Whenever possible, check your baggage at curbside.

Don't struggle with heavy baggage on public transportation to save a couple of dollars. Hire a cab, and tip the cabbie.

Rent a Table Many business meetings can be and are conducted over a table in a hotel dining room. If you are planning to linger long at a meal, let the maitre d' or hostess know in advance and also advise your waiter. Be prepared to tip generously. The amount you spend will still be considerably less than the cost of a meeting room in the same facility.

If you want a prime table for one as you travel alone, be prepared to tip for it.

Hotel Services Don't get yourself in a frenzy over your schedule or your possessions. Ask the hotel valet, concierge, or housekeeping to help you. Tip well. It will be worth what you spend.

A Case Study One traveler had to make back-to-back trips to a major city. Each stay was for three days. The first trip she tipped generously and availed herself of help from others. She ate average-priced meals in full-service restaurants and took cabs. The total cost of the trip was $1,385, including air fare.

The second trip she decided to go it alone. She carried her own bags, ate at cafeterias several times, and used public transportation rather than cabs. She stayed at the same hotel, however, and the air fare was the same, as was the overall schedule of flights and appointments. In going it alone, she truly wanted to see how little she could spend on the trip. The "no frills" trip cost $1,315.

The difference between the two trips was enormous—far more than the $70 price tag. She returned home from the first trip feeling relaxed, upbeat, and ready to resume work in the home office. After the second trip, she felt absolutely exhausted and more than a little uptight. She had a muscle strain in one shoulder (a painful condition that took several weeks to heal). The $70 in savings went for a physician's appointment and subsequent medication.

Rule of Thumb   A simple rule of thumb: if others can help you on your trip, let them.

39 ✈ Carry On a Day's Supply

Every traveler has different personal needs. Ask yourself, What is the one thing that I can least do without for twenty-four hours?

Special Necessities To a person who needs medication daily (for example, heart medication), it will be an ample supply of medicine.

To a person with diabetes, it will be insulin. If you are insulin-dependent, plan to carry your supplies with you as part of your carry-on luggage (never checked), and make sure that you have *more* than the amount you will need.

To a person who wears glasses or contact lenses, it will be the ability to see. Take along an extra pair of prescription eyewear in case you lose or break your glasses or contacts.

The Basics To most people, it will be soap, a toothbrush, and a comb. Carry these items with you in your briefcase, purse, or the carry-on bag that you have close to you at all times.

Also pack in your carry-on bag

- basic makeup supplies.

- feminine protection.

- an extra pair of underwear.

- an extra pair of socks or hosiery.

Just in Case The fact is, you never know for sure when your flight might be diverted, the road might be closed, the bridge might be washed out, or your luggage might not arrive when you do.

Be prepared to live out of your carry-on bag for at least twenty-four hours.

Be prepared in your overall planning for your trip to be extended a day or two. You never know when a flight may be canceled, weather may detain you, or you may need the extra day on the road to close a major deal or complete a sale.

40 ✈ Maintain Your Temperature

Too-hot or too-cold temperatures are not only un-comfortable and frustrating, but they can lead to illness or emergency situations (from heat exhaustion to frostbite). Here are twelve practical tips for maintaining your ideal temperature.

First, Dress Properly for the Environment to Which You Are Going If you are leaving the snow of Chicago for the warmth of Phoenix, dress for Phoenix, and then put on a heavy topcoat, scarf, and gloves. That way, you can acclimate to Phoenix weather within seconds.

Ask about the weather before you pack. Consult national weather forecasts or newspapers that give national or international weather predictions. Ask your travel agent about what kind of weather you can expect in a foreign city.

Second, Dress in Layers You'll get more warmth out of a shirt or blouse, a sweater vest, a jacket, and a coat than out of a wool top and a down jacket because warm air will be trapped between the layers of clothing to give you greater insulation. Plan and develop your wardrobe with layering possibilities in mind.

Third, Don't Suffer If you're hot, take something off. If you're cold, put something on.

Fourth, Always Carry One More Layer with You Carry a sweater or lightweight jacket with you. Many people tend to get cold on planes or in theaters or restaurants.

Fifth, Avoid Sitting or Sleeping in Drafts on the Plane, in Restaurants, or in Your Hotel Turn off the air-control knob before you sleep on a plane. There should be enough circulation without having the air blow directly on your face or neck.

Sixth, Sleep Cool If you have a choice between sleeping in an overly hot room or an overly cool one, choose the cool room, and ask for extra blankets.

Seventh, Consider Taking Along a Fabric Shawl One traveler's all-time favorite travel garment is actually a double-thick piece of thin high-quality wool thirty inches wide and five feet long, fringed at each end. She has slept under this "blanket," has used this "scarf" to fight against severe winds (wearing it over the head or wrapped around the neck), and has worn this fabric strip as a shawl-style vest crisscrossed under a coat.

Eighth, Ask for an Adjustment If you can't figure out how to control the temperature in your hotel room, ask for assistance. If you are uncomfortable in a restaurant, let your waiter know it and perhaps ask to be reseated. If you are roasting in the back of a cab, ask the driver to roll down the windows or turn on the air-conditioning.

Ninth, Drink Plenty of Fluids One of the best ways to avoid getting overly heated or to keep from freezing is to keep fluids moving through your body. Allow yourself to perspire. It's nature's way of cooling you off.

Tenth, Use Ice Cubes or Cold Water to Get Cool in Equatorial Climates To get cool quickly, place cold packs of ice across your wrists or the inside of each forearm, or immerse your hands—up to your elbows—in cold water. An ice pack on the back of the neck is also helpful. (Make sure it reaches around to cover the arteries on the sides of the neck.)

Eleventh, Wear a Hat If you are going to a hot climate, take along a hat that breathes, such as a straw or loosely woven hat. If you are going to a cold climate, take along a hat that can be pulled down over the ears.

Twelfth, Dress a Little More Lightly Than You Would in Your Office Travel requires more physical exertion than regular activities.

Remember these general rules:

- You can always put on more clothing, but you can only take off so much.

- It's easier to get warm than to get cool.

41 ✈ Take Along a Medicine Kit

"Don't forget to take your pills" is good advice for travelers, too.

Prescriptions If you take prescription medicines, pack a sufficient quantity and a few extra doses, too, in case of a travel delay or change in itinerary.

Think ahead. Plan to have all the medications you need in hand several days in advance of leaving for your trip.

Information and Instructions If you are under a physician's care for a major illness or chronic ailment, it's a good idea to take along an information sheet (packed into your case on a permanent basis or tucked into your wallet) that lists your physician's name and phone numbers, the names and phone numbers of specialists you see regularly, the name and phone number of your hospital, and all the prescription medications that you take on an ongoing basis—including dosages and frequency.

General First Aid Even if you don't take prescription medicine, you'll probably want to take along a basic first aid kit that will include the following items:

- A painkiller, such as aspirin, Tylenol, or Advil

- An antacid or alkaline product to neutralize stomach acid (such as Alka-Seltzer, Tums, Rolaids, Digel)

- A product to treat diarrhea

- Nose drops

- An assortment of bandages

- A small bottle of antiseptic (or peroxide)

- Q-tips

- Cold medications (decongestant, antihistamine)

- Throat lozenges

- Motion sickness tablets

Look for travel sizes of products you normally take or for packages with individually wrapped pills or capsules.

If you are going to be outside a great deal, take along a sunblock.

If you are going into a wilderness area, you'll probably want to take an insect repellent.

If you are going overseas, you'll probably want to take water purification tablets. In some cases, a physician will prescribe a general antibiotic for you to take along, too.

Remember to take along your vitamins, also.

Bottles and Labels   It's a good idea to take prescription medications with you in the bottles or containers in which you received them from the pharmacy. That way, you'll avoid getting confused along the way, and should you become ill, others will be able to help you more effectively. The containers, of course, give the names of your pharmacy and physician—that's useful information for others to have should you become unconscious or should customs officials question you about the pills in your possession.

42 ✈ Personal Safety Tips

Travel hubs—such as airport terminals, especially international terminals, train stations, bus stations, and docks—are favorite places of thieves.

Always carry any valuables on your person in the safest way possible. Shoulder bags are safer than clutch or short-strapped purses. They are best carried around the neck, with the bag itself carried in front of the body instead of toward the back. Make sure your purse, briefcase, or carry-on bag can be secured, usually with zippers. Open-top tote bags and purses should be left at home.

Don't lay a wallet and keys on a countertop while you rummage through your purse or bags.

Keep money, tickets, and your passport in a folder that can be stored in a carry-on bag or carried in an interior coat pocket that has a button enclosure or flap. Never carry your wallet, tickets, or passport in a back pocket.

In Your Hotel   Make certain that you use the safety locks on doors and windows. Open your door only to persons you are expecting. If you question the identity of a person at your door, ask to see identification before opening the door fully.

Ever Alert   The best safety advice is to remain alert at all times. Don't let yourself daydream as you move through an unfamiliar environment. Take note of people, places, and things. Know where you're going, and walk and act with boldness and certainty. Muggers tend to pick on people who show hesitancy, timidity, or frailty.

If you suspect that you are being followed, move immediately into a well-lit public area. When walking on city sidewalks, stay as close to the curb as possible. If you suspect danger in walking on a city street, cross the street, or even walk into the street. If you have any qualms about entering an elevator, don't enter it. If you have an uneasy feeling about getting off an elevator, don't get off. Ride it to the top and stop at your floor on the way down or, if necessary, return to the lobby.

Even before leaving a hotel lobby for your room, have your key or entry card in hand before you get on an elevator.

Other Tips   Stay in reputable places.

Dress modestly. Try to blend in with those around you. Wearing neutral colors and avoiding flashy jewelry will help you maintain a low profile.

Remember these tips:

- Light is your friend. Stay in well-lit places; park in well-lit parking places.

- There's safety in numbers. Stay in public places.

- Noise is your best weapon. If you suspect trouble or begin to experience a problem, honk the horn, scream, yell, or do what you must to make as much noise as possible.

On the Road Don't pull over at the insistence of another driver (except a police officer). Don't lower your car window more than a couple of inches when speaking to a stranger from your car. If you experience car trouble, stay in your car, and post a sign asking fellow travelers to call for assistance on your behalf. Keep your business car well maintained.

Personal Safety Courses If you are a woman who travels a great deal, you may find it beneficial and confidence building to take a course in personal safety. Your local police department can suggest such programs to you.

43 ✈ Secure the Home Front

You need to think about two worlds—the one in which you are moving, and the one you have left behind. Home-front concerns don't disappear once a business trip begins. In many cases, they become more intensified!

General Tips Consider having your paycheck deposited directly to your bank account, and then arrange for direct payment of bills that are the same amount each month, such as health insurance, mortgage or rent, loan repayment amounts, and installment payments.

Give power of attorney to someone who can conduct business in your name and on your behalf should you be detained or should you or your family experience a crisis.

The Traveler with a Family Be sure to leave word or instructions with other members of your family about home repair or home maintenance services that you have requested to be done while you are away. Alert your family to any items you have ordered that might be delivered while you're gone. Be sure to leave your set of car keys with your spouse (unless you are leaving your car at the airport).

If you're a traveling mom, refuse to come home to a filthy house or stacks of dirty dishes and laundry. If you must work in a job that requires travel, insist that your family take responsibility for doing the chores that you would otherwise do if you were at home.

The Traveler Who Is Single If you are single and you travel extensively, you will probably want to

- have your mail delivered to a post office box. That way, you avoid a lot of stop-order requests and the need for getting to the post office during business hours to pick up mail.

- have your newspaper and magazines delivered to your place of business or plan to buy your newspaper and magazines from newsstands.

- avoid investing in lots of living house plants.

- postpone your acquisition of a house pet.

Make a checklist to secure your home before you leave:

- Empty the trash. Don't let rotting garbage attract bugs or rodents in your absence.

- Wash the dishes. Don't come home to dried-on grime.

- Water the house plants (depending, of course, on how long you are planning to be away).

- Turn off all electrical appliances that need to be turned off. Consider unplugging your television set and any electronics equipment that could suffer from a power surge. Make it a habit to unplug all small appliances (such as curling irons, steam irons, and toaster ovens) when you are not using them.

- Lower the thermostat in winter, or raise it in summer. There's no reason to pay for heat or air-conditioning you aren't enjoying.

- Leave the cabinet doors under sinks cracked open a bit, or make sure that outside pipes are wrapped should you be traveling in winter. Disconnect outside garden hoses if you suspect a hard freeze during your absence.

44 ✈ Anticipating a Vehicle Emergency

In anticipating an emergency, you are not expecting one to happen, but you are anticipating what your response would be in case of an emergency. In some ways, you are mentally rehearsing a safe escape.

Air and Train Travel When choosing where to sit on an airplane or train, choose to sit close to an exit or an emergency exit. Choose an aisle seat, which allows you the greatest flexibility to get up and move quickly in case of emergency. Visually locate the nearest exit, and count the number of rows between you and that row. (In case of dense smoke, you'll be able to feel your way to the exit with greater accuracy.)

Emergency exit rows have an added advantage in that those sitting in the next row forward cannot recline their seats—which generally means a little more room for those sitting in emergency exit rows.

Keep your seat belt secured as you travel by airplane.

Car Travel   If you are taking a business trip by car,

- be sure to take along a roadside emergency kit, including jumper cables, flares, and a "Please Call for Help" sign.

- take along a blanket. Even if it isn't winter, a blanket can be useful in times of accident, especially to help victims of shock.

- keep a first aid kit in your car.

- have a set of tire chains if you are traveling in winter or anticipate traveling to areas where you may encounter snowfall or mud slides.

- keep a container of water in the car. Take along extra water if you are traveling through deserts.

- use your seat belt.

- double-check your tires, all hoses and belts, and fluid levels in advance of your trip.

Take these documents with you as you travel by car:

1. Your driver's license
2. Your vehicle registration form
3. Proof of insurance coverage
4. The owner's manual for your car

Travel by Ship   If you are traveling by ship, know at all times the location of the nearest life preservers and life boats (or rafts). Mentally rehearse a way out of your ship's cabin should lights be unavailable. Familiarize yourself with the location of the nearest emergency signaling devices.

45 ✈ When in Doubt, Ask

Don't waste time or mental and emotional energy if you have questions you can't answer. Ask!

How to Get There? If you need directions, ask for them.

If you get lost, ask for assistance.

If you have difficulty interpreting a map or schedule in a travel center, ask for clarification from someone who works in the terminal or at a ticket counter.

If you don't know how to use the public transportation system (bus routes, subway routes), ask for help at an information desk before leaving the terminal, depot, or hotel lobby.

How Much? If you don't know how much to tip, ask for advice from the person to whom you want to give the tip. Simply ask, "What is the average tip that you receive?" Nearly all persons in service professions will be honest with you. (They'd rather you ask and leave a tip than not leave a suitable tip because you didn't know what was appropriate!)

If you question the amount you are being

charged for goods or services, ask for clarification or a written statement.

What's the Custom? If you don't know what to wear to a meeting or event, ask your hostess (or the person issuing the invitation). If you aren't sure what black tie means, ask specifically, "What does black tie entail in this community?"

If you don't know the custom or acceptable cultural norm, ask your colleagues in the city or your hotel concierge.

How Does It Work? If you don't know how to operate something (whether it's turning off the heat in your hotel room, turning on the television set, using the phone, or flushing the toilet), ask for help.

You'll rarely be discredited for asking. On the contrary, those around you will probably think you are wise and sensitive in asking.

You can learn a lot, of course, just by watching others. Be an observer of your fellow travelers.

46 ✈ Do Your Homework

Just as you will no doubt have done your business homework before the meeting, interview, or appointment you are facing, so, too, you'll find it advantageous to do your homework about the non-business environment.

Know Who Know as much as possible about persons with whom you will be meeting, to whom you will be speaking or listening, or from whom you will be soliciting an order.

Know a little about

- their personal backgrounds.
- their likes and dislikes.
- their relationship with others with whom you are doing, or have done, business.
- their positions in the company.
- their abilities to make decisions.

You can get this information from your colleagues, from others who have done business with the persons in the past, or from the persons themselves (usually in a nonbusiness setting). Express a sincere interest in the lives of those with whom you will be dealing. Even if you aren't successful in closing a deal on this trip, you will have laid the foundation for a relationship that may have very positive results down the line.

Know Where   Before you make a presentation, or as you begin attending a convention, scout out the area in which your meeting is scheduled. Get your bearings. Where is the meeting room? How is it arranged? Where are the nearest rest room, drinking fountain, vending machine, and telephone? In what part of town are you located? What are the best routes to take to the facility and within the facility?

If you are in another state or nation, know where you are in proximity to major cities, common points of reference, borders, or zones within a city.

Know What   Learn as much as possible about the culture in which you are conducting business. Culture is not an area limited to foreign travel. Ask such questions as these:

- What language will be spoken? Will interpreters be used? By whom will they be provided? If the language is one you know or one you speak marginally, will you be expected to speak in the language of the meeting? Do you speak the jargon required? Are you adept at using the terms known by others in the meeting or conference?

- What are the body language norms? Do you shake hands or bow? If you bow, how low? How close are you expected to stand? Will you be looking the other person in the eye or standing next to the person so that you both are looking out at the world?

- What is the expected protocol—the order of procession, the order of seating, the means of introduction, the appropriate dress, the proper table manners, the signal that a session is over?

Know When   Get a feel in advance for how the people with whom you are meeting regard time. Don't become upset if your appointment is postponed or delayed. Instead, take along something to do during the wait. Respond to the meeting in a timely manner but with regard to the culture. Is a next-day follow-up call acceptable? Can you wait until you get home to gather the information needed, or should you call home immediately and have the information gathered and faxed to you?

47 ✦ Schedule Windup and Unwind Time

Your business trip actually begins when you start gathering all of the things you will need to take on your trip—both at work and at home. (Windup time includes the time it takes to get the haircut, have the prescription filled, pick up the clothes from the cleaners, and take the dog to the kennel.) A business trip officially ends when you have unpacked your bags and have processed all of the things related to the trip (including cleaning dirty clothes, taking luggage or shoes to repair, filing expense account reports, and writing follow-up or debriefing letters, reports, and memos).

Overcoming Jetlag The time needed to overcome jetlag should be a part of your business trip schedule. Don't expect to come home from the Orient or Europe at eight o'clock one night and jump right back into your regular office routine at eight o'clock the next morning. You won't be at your best. In fact, you may not even be coherent enough to conduct good business. It's better to get the rest you need and then reappear in the office at full speed.

Back in Town or Back in the Office?
When scheduling a business trip, let your associates know when they can expect you back in the office, not necessarily when you will be back in town.

The Overall Pattern   If you take only one or two business trips a year, the few hours that you rob yourself of needed rest and relaxation probably aren't going to matter a great deal. But if you travel frequently, regularly, and for long stretches at a time, you *must* learn to schedule windup and unwind time as a part of your business trips in order to maintain

- your personal balance between home and work.

- your energy levels, both physically and mentally.

- your willingness to keep traveling.

- your creativity.

The traveler who allows weekends to be consumed with work travel is no different from the employee who works on weekends while at home. Both burn out quickly.

Playing on the Road Is Different   Some travelers attempt to convince themselves that because they take time out to play while on the road

—a round of golf perhaps or a theater performance one evening—they are getting the away-
from-work time that they need to maintain a
healthy balance. On-the-road playtime isn't the
same as at-home playtime. Recreation on the road
usually takes the form of an event or yet another
experience. Recreation at home is usually a
nonevent, a time of doing nothing.

The moments of exercise, levity, and fun on the
road rarely provide the total rest that can be experienced only in an environment that is completely
comfortable and undemanding—in other words, at
home.

48 ✦ Be Positive About Travel

Approach your opportunity to travel on business with a positive frame of mind.

Seeing the Benefits of Being Positive In staying positive, you'll find that you have more energy and creativity to pour into your business ventures, which means that your business travel is likely to yield greater rewards than it might otherwise. You'll also experience less stress and pressure in coming home.

Maintaining a Positive Attitude As you travel,

- see humor along the way. It may be in what you do, in what others around you do, or in the general absurdities of life. Allow yourself to laugh.

- see your business opportunities as a personal opportunity for growth to learn more about cities and nations, about cultures and languages, about your business and business in general, about people and human behaviors common to us all, and about travel itself. Don't simply be an observer of the world as you pass through it. Be a student of life.

• stay curious. Ask yourself frequently, What does this mean? What processes are at work here? Who is in control and why? How does this relate to me? How can I use this information? Travel can lead to great creative ideas as well as to profound insights.

Keeping Travel Positive for Your Family
Your business travel can provide growth opportunities for your family members.

Share with your family the information, insights, and experiences that you have. Expand the horizons of your children. Tell them the stories that you hear along the way and the lessons that you are learning.

Also point out ways in which your family members are compelled to grow as individuals because you are away from home. No doubt they will learn new skills, become more independent, and become more adept at solving problems and making decisions on the basis of their own information gathering. They will need to grow in their ability to take responsibility. Not all of these lessons are easily learned or acquired without pain. The fact is, however, that these lessons would not be easily or painlessly learned if you were at home; the lessons would only be delayed.

If your children need to be left in the care of baby-sitters while you are away on business, speak highly of the sitters you hire. Point out to your children the opportunity they have to meet somebody new.

49 ✈ Don't Use Travel as an Escape

Don't let business travel become an excuse for leaving behind unresolved issues at home. Avoid saying, "We'll talk about it when I get back," or "We'll deal with it when I return."

Choose to communicate about a problem *before* you leave on a business trip, even if you need to stay up half the night to do so. Come to a point of resolution. Of course, you don't have to solve the problem. You just need to come to some point of agreement about action to take (now and later).

Choose to deal with negative situations as they arise. Don't put them off.

The fact is, you might as well deal with the problem before you leave because you won't truly be able to leave it behind you anyway. The unresolved problem will dog you the entire business trip, no doubt growing in magnitude and stress level, until you may start dreading to come home. Don't let that happen! Clear the interpersonal family air before you leave, and keep the air clear as you travel.

On-the-Road Discipline Don't relinquish your position of authority in the family when you go away on business. Come to an agreement with your spouse that your from-the-road disciplinary actions carry just as much weight in your absence as if you were at home.

Quality Communication   If a problem arises while you are away, get to the root of it over the phone. Learn how to communicate at deep levels over the phone: ask questions that cause family members to open up to you and share with you how they are truly feeling, what they are fearing or dreading, and how they are responding to the situations around them. Talk over decisions. Let your spouse know that you feel responsible for what happens at home and that you want to be involved.

Daily Involvement   Know what your children are facing in their lives—their events, their games, their recitals, their lessons, their exams—and express interest daily in what your children are doing and thinking.

The Big Picture   If you and your spouse never seem to have time to talk about the children when you are together—perhaps because you are too busy talking to them—use your travel conversations to talk about the broad trends you see in your children's development. Talk over specific ideas about things you both can do to further their growth spiritually, emotionally, and mentally.

At Home When you are at home, be fully at home with your family. Play with them. Work with them. Listen to them. Let them know how much you like coming home to them. In communicating with your family while you are at home, you lay the groundwork for more successful communication with them while you are away.

50 ✝ Pray for Your Family

Before you leave on a business trip, call the family together and have a time of prayer.

Pray for Your Family Pray for the protection, well-being, health, and wisdom of each family member in your absence. Call each person's name in prayer and ask God to be with family members in a special way—to help them do what is right, mind the person left in charge (whether your spouse or a baby-sitter), and feel your love even across the miles.

Ask God to guard and protect your home and the comings and goings of your family members. Ask God to lead you all into the paths in which you should walk and to deliver you from harm.

Pray specifically about the challenges your spouse and children will be facing in your absence:

- Your children's relationships with friends and teachers

- Your spouse's work and relationships within the family, the church, and the community

- The specific tests that will occur while you are away—school exams, sports games, try-outs and auditions, and interviews

Receive Your Family's Prayers   Ask your family to pray for you. Let each child give voice to prayer on your behalf—for your safety, for those you will meet and with whom you will work, for wisdom as you make decisions, for your health, for the successful completion of the business at hand.

Anticipate Good Results   As you pray together, anticipate with joy the time when you will all be together again. Anticipate blessings and opportunities that will come your way during the days ahead—for you on the road and for your family at home. Encourage your children to be on the alert for God's insights and miracles in your absence, and let them know that you will anticipate hearing about them.

Pray on the Road   Pray for your family while you're on the road and keep them close in your heart and mind. Periodically, write a letter about spiritual matters. Being away will afford you a special opportunity to reflect from a distance.

Let your children know how pleased you are with their growth and development, and especially about their relationship with God. Share with them your hopes and dreams for their lives—not necessarily specific things you hope they will do, but the quality and character of the lives they will live as productive, loving adults.

Pray Back at Home   When you return home, give thanks for God's protection and provision while you were apart. Share with one another the ways in which you felt God's presence binding your hearts together.

51 ✈ Be Kind to Those You Meet Along the Way

It's true that you may never see them again on this earth, you may never know their names, and the seconds, minutes, or hours you spend with them may seem of little immediate consequence. It's also true, however, that your fellow travelers can and do affect your life.

Be kind to those with whom you travel. Speak to them positively. Compliment them. Smile at them. Be courteous to them. In 90 percent of the cases, you'll receive from them what you give: positive words, appreciation, smiles, and courtesy.

Ask About the Other Person's Profession Learn a little about what it's like to do the person's job, the obstacles and challenges faced, the personal sense of fulfillment in the work, and the way in which business is conducted in the profession. You will broaden your general understanding about the world, and you may pick up some valuable tips that apply to the way in which you personally conduct your business affairs.

Ask Where the Other Person Is From—Both Now and Originally Find out what you can about the city in which the person lives. You may be called upon to do business in that city someday! Ask about what it was like to grow up where the person grew up—the customs, the traditions, the general environment. What do you share in common? If the person is significantly older or younger than you are, ask about how times have changed or about what is currently "in" among folks of the person's age. You can learn a lot about the very broad topic we all share in common: human behavior.

Are you sitting next to a young child? Ask about school, heroes, likes and dislikes. You may be amazed at what you discover about the younger generation.

Ask if the Person Has Ever Been to the City in Which You Are Traveling   If so, is there a favorite place, a favorite restaurant, a favorite memory? Is there something you should see, do, try, eat, order, or experience? Where's the favorite place to attend church, shop, jog, or watch a sunrise? What local customs should you watch out for? What local issues are hot? What are the main concerns of the people in the city? You can learn a lot about the place.

See People as People   Whether fellow travelers or those who belong to a place, see people as individual people, not as obstacles around which you must move in life. When you see others as individuals, they see you as an individual. And as a result, you'll enjoy your trip more.

Have a Helpful Attitude   Help others whenever you can—for example, to find directions, to get assistance, to board a bus, to hail a cab. Do what you can to make their trip a little easier. Even if the person can do nothing for you in return, others around you will be influenced by your helping. They, in turn, will be more positive toward you or toward others. In all, you'll be doing something to make the world a friendlier place.

Take on the road with you the attitude of care that you know to be valuable at home. Seek to be a peacemaker in a troubled world.

52 ✈ Say So . . . Even Across the Miles

Don't let the miles silence your emotions or opinions. Give voice to your inner self as you travel. Be a real person, not a caricature, to those you have left at home.

Express Your Love Keep your love for your family kindled. Tell members of your family that you love them—in either spoken or written word. Don't let your family members wonder how you feel about them while you are away. Tell them! Write an occasional love letter to each member of your family. Be concrete in expressing what you value about the other person and how you feel when you are apart.

Voice Your Concerns Are you angry about something that you perceive has gone awry in our world? Wax philosophical occasionally, and let your family know what worries you, troubles you, upsets you, irritates you, angers you, or frustrates you about the age in which we live. Let your family see you as being involved with the world—the whole world with all of its political, social, cultural, and economic facets.

Reveal Who You Are Be genuinely yourself in your letters and phone calls, and attempt to express the whole of yourself to those you value back at home. As a traveler, you'll have a little different perspective on the world from that of persons who always stay in the neighborhood. Share that perspective with your family as fully as you can.

If you keep a travel journal, record your innermost thoughts. Periodically share from that journal with your family.

Admit Your Longings and Weaknesses Do you miss your family sometimes to the point of tears? Let them know it. They will think of you not as being weak but as being tender and as being even more lovable.

Share Victories and Defeats Have you had a great day? Say so. Has the day been the pits? Admit it. Don't paint a gloomy picture of life on the road; at the same time, don't create the illusion that life on the road is a party. Be realistic with your family, and share with them both the joys and the disappointments. Share with your family the hopes and dreams that you have, and give them an insight periodically into why you feel the need to be away from them. Do you have a goal—a reason for working so hard and long away from the family? Express that goal to your family. Involve them in the goal. Help your children and spouse to see themselves as partners in a mutual endeavor (which happens to require travel on your part).

It's natural when you are away from your family for your family members to imagine you for better or for worse. In some cases, they'll idealize you. At other times, they may hate you for being away. The more, however, that you share with your family members the way you feel—day to day, week to week, trip to trip—the more they'll come to see you and know you as a three-dimensional, flesh-and-blood, genuine person. In other words, the more they'll know *you*.

And the more they know you, the more they'll be comfortable with your presence and with your absence.